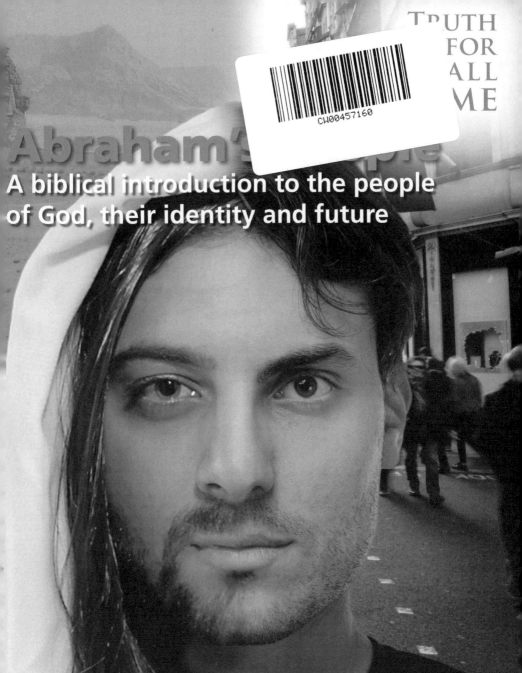

TRUTH
FOR
ALL
TIME

Abraham's People

A biblical introduction to the people of God, their identity and future

Malcolm Jones

Day One

ENDORSEMENTS

This concise and straightforward book will help readers grasp the unity of the Bible story and God's plan of salvation for his people. Malcolm Jones writes as someone who was raised in dispensationalism but came to see that the promises God made to Israel have been fulfilled in Christ for all who come to faith in him. Jewish and Gentile Christians alike are heirs of these promises and look forward together to a glorious eternal inheritance. This book would be ideal to help new and confused Christians understand the complex relationship between the Old and the New Testament, and provides a valuable non-technical introduction to basic biblical theology. It is easy to read and accessible, thoroughly biblical and mercifully free of intimidating academic references and footnotes. The outline of Paul's argument in Romans 9–11 is especially lucid and convincing.

John Stevens, National Director, Fellowship of Independent Evangelical Churches

The nobles of the nations assemble
as the people of the God of Abraham.'
Psalm 47:9

'If you belong to Christ, then you are Abraham's seed, and
heirs according to the promise.'
Galatians 3:29

Contents

To be reared in a Christian home is a great privilege, and I will always be grateful to my parents for bringing me up 'in the training and instruction of the Lord'. However, to remain within the confines of one's own Christian tradition, and to disown all others, is inevitably to imbibe without questioning the teachings and distinctives of the group.

Within the circle to which I belonged, Dr C. I. Scofield and his version of dispensationalism was highly revered. The notes printed below the text in his reference Bible were assigned almost the same authority as the Bible text itself.

As a result, for more than the first thirty years of my life, I believed that the Bible was not one book, but two. Along with that, I believed that the Bible focused on two different peoples: Israel, God's earthly people; and the church, God's heavenly people.

This, of course, necessitated two gospels (in fact, we found a number of gospels)! This went along with seeing the Old Testament as a book of law and the New Testament as a book of grace.

Inevitably, there had to be two kingdoms—one an earthly kingdom ruled over by Jews, and the other a heavenly kingdom which one entered by being born again.

The hopes of these two communities had to be similarly distinct, the hope of Israel being earthly and the hope of the church being spiritual, to be realized by a 'secret rapture'.

Although I had seemingly been well acquainted with Hebrews 11, I still remember the day when verses 13–16 hit me between the eyes. I recall the profound shock of discovering that the Old Testament people of faith were, like me, 'foreigners and strangers on earth'; that the country they were looking forward to inhabiting did not consist in some real estate in the Middle East, but 'a better country—a heavenly one'.

How could these supposedly 'earthly people' have had the same heavenly hope which I had? How could the writer of Hebrews affirm that, while many of his heroes in the chapter lived in Canaan, 'none of them received what had been promised' (v. 39)? How could he conclude the chapter by saying that 'only together with us [Christian believers] would they be made perfect'?

The Bible suddenly became a new book for me. It was saying things I had overlooked or ignored for decades. There was a divine plan to it—a single, united plan—'to bring unity to all things in heaven and on earth under Christ' (Eph. 1:10). I found that in the eternal city to come, the names of the twelve tribes of Israel are on its gates and the names of the twelve apostles of the Lamb are on its foundation stones; and what God has joined together no one will be able to 'put asunder'.

This book is an attempt to share the wonder of the Scriptures in all their glorious unity, and to glorify Christ through whom the eternal plan will come to its rich fulfilment. 'For from him and through him and for him are all things. To him be the glory for ever! Amen' (Rom. 11:36).

One book

The Bible in front of me has a blank page separating Matthew from Malachi. Someone has called it the only page in the Bible that isn't divinely inspired. More than that, before I begin at Matthew chapter 1, I'm told that I'm embarking on the 'New Testament'. All that comes before Matthew is 'Old Testament'.

Instinctively that forces me to think in terms of two books, not one. More than that, it makes me (being a child of my age) think that the 'Old' has to be in some way inferior to the 'New'. Does what is 'New' not replace what is 'Old'? Does not what is 'Old' belong to a past generation somewhere? Surely the 'New' is what I should be looking at! As I am a 'new creation' in Christ (2 Cor. 5:17), what has the 'Old' Testament got to do with me?

One interlocking book

In fact, the Bible is like a symphony in two parts or a play in two acts. If we only stay for the first half of the performance, we leave dissatisfied. We feel and know there must be more to come. It is incomplete and therefore only makes partial sense. On the other hand, if we don't arrive until Part 2 commences, we are confused. We need an explanation as to how the masterpiece reached the point at which we came in.

Matthew begins his Gospel narrative with the words, 'This is the genealogy of Jesus the Messiah the son of David, the son of Abraham.' But who were David and Abraham? Which lived first? Why is it important that Jesus be a descendant of those men? We wouldn't know if we didn't read Part 1—the Old Testament. How can non-Jewish Christians know what Paul meant when he talked about Jesus Christ as 'our Passover lamb' (1 Cor. 5:7)? Only by reading the Old Testament. Similarly, how can we identify the promised deliverer—the one who would crush the serpent (Gen. 3:15), gain 'the obedience of the nations' (Gen. 49:10), be born in Bethlehem (Micah 5:2) to a virgin mother (Isa. 7:14), be 'pierced for our transgressions' (Isa. 53:5), and be exalted as King and Priest (Ps. 110:1–4)? Only by reading the New Testament.

One divine Author

By any criterion, the Bible is a remarkable book. It was written by more than forty people (ranging from kings, prophets and poets to shepherds and fishermen), in three languages, over some twenty-five centuries in many different locations. And yet, what unites these documents into one is that they have the same divine Author.

Each of the writers 'spoke from God as they were carried along by the Holy Spirit' (2 Peter 1:21). The Holy Spirit speaks through the Old Testament writers (Acts 1:16; 4:25; 28:25; Heb.3:7–11; 10:15–17) as much as through the New Testament writers (1 Cor. 14:37; 1 John 4:6; Rev. 2:7, etc.). Both 'Old' and 'New' are referred to simply as 'Scripture' (see 2 Tim. 3:15; 2 Peter 3:16). Whether he is quoting from Moses or Luke, Paul refers to the writings of both as 'Scripture' (1 Tim. 5:18), for the Bible is one book—God's book.

One complete book

Not only is the Bible one book with one Author, it is also one complete book. By that, I mean that we shouldn't be looking for further revelations than those given in it. We certainly need to pray for greater illumination to understand what is written there, but we must avoid any claim of supplementary authoritative revelation, whether from the Book of Mormon, the Qur'an, or a self-appointed Christian prophet.

Peter went to his reward not encouraging his readers to expect new revelations from God. He urged them 'to recall the words spoken in the past by the holy prophets and the command given by our Lord and

Saviour through your apostles' (2 Peter 3:2). Notice how he brings the Old and New Testaments together. The task given by Paul the apostle to his young colleague Timothy was not to add to what he had learned from the apostle, but to 'keep' and 'guard the good deposit' and entrust it 'to reliable people who will also be qualified to teach others' (2 Tim. 1:13–14; 2:2; see also Jude 3). It is noteworthy that the Bible's final warning is not to add to or subtract from what is written (Rev. 22:18–19).

One Christian book

If the Bible is one book, written by one Author, to whom does it belong? Should it be the property of the synagogue or of the church? Let's answer those questions by asking two more.

The first question is this: For whom was the Bible written? Obviously there is a very simple answer to that question if we are thinking only of the New Testament. But we are not. We have argued that 'Old' and 'New' Testaments together form one book. So, for whom was the Old Testament written? Some people will say that it was written for Jews and that it is a Jewish book. But what does the New Testament have to say on the matter? It has a very clear answer, which it gives a number of times.

For example, writing to the Christian churches in Rome, Paul says this about what we call 'the Old Testament': 'For everything that was written in the past was written to teach *us*, so that through the endurance taught in the Scriptures and the encouragement they provide *we* might have hope' (Rom. 15:4; cf. 4:23–24).[1] Writing to predominantly Gentile Christians, Paul says that the ancient Scriptures were written for *our* instruction, so that *we* might have hope. He confirms that view to another largely non-Jewish church, by pointing out that the history of Israel in the wilderness was 'written down as warnings for *us*, on whom the culmination of the ages has come' (1 Cor. 10:11).

According to Peter, the Old Testament prophets were aware of this. He says, 'It was revealed to them that they were not serving themselves but you [Christians], when they spoke of the things that have now been told you by those who have preached the gospel to you …' (1 Peter 1:12).

So the entire Bible was written for Christian people from all nations.

The second question is: To whom shall we turn for a right understanding of the Scriptures? If the Old Testament was a Jewish book, the obvious thing might be to listen to Jewish interpreters of it. However, neither history nor Scripture encourages us to do that. When the Lord Jesus was here, he found Israel's leaders to be mostly in the dark when it came to understanding what was written. Though they trusted in Moses, they didn't actually believe him (John 5:46–47). The Sadducees were charged by Jesus with not knowing the Scriptures (Matt. 22:29), and even Nicodemus (though 'the teacher of Israel') was ignorant about the need to be born again (John 3:10).

Before running too quickly to Jewish scholars for an understanding of Scripture, we need to note Paul's caution that 'Even to this day when Moses is read, a veil covers their hearts' (2 Cor. 3:15–16).

How is that veil taken away? By turning to the Lord! He is the authoritative interpreter of the Old Testament, as he is the illuminator of it to his people (Luke 24:27, 32, 44–45). It has been helpfully noted that, 'though we read the Bible forwards, we understand it backwards'. And we do so because we must read the Scriptures through the eyes of Christ and his apostles. If we fail to do this, our understanding of the Old Testament may satisfy Jews or Moslems, but only because we haven't allowed Christ to lift the veil from our hearts. After all, it was written about him. And it was all written down for us, if we are Christian believers.

But, though the whole Bible was written *for* us, was it all written *about* us? That's our next question.

NOTES

1   All italics in Scripture quotes throughout this book have been added for emphasis.

One people

The idea has surfaced a number of times that God has two families—Israel and the church. The first is thought of as God's earthly people, and the second as his heavenly people. National Israel is still reckoned by some to be God's chosen people—even though its citizens are predominantly atheistic—alongside the church.

Leaving aside the serious difficulty as to how atheists can be thought of as part of God's people, let's ask ourselves whether the Scriptures support such a position. Do they present us with two peoples owned by God, or one? Who are the true children of Abraham?

John and Jesus

The first surprise we encounter in our investigation is that being one of Abraham's true offspring is not a matter of nationality. That hits us at a very early stage in the New Testament. John the Baptist was disturbed by the arrival of Pharisees and Sadducees at the place where he was baptizing. Rather than flatter Israel's religious establishment, he called their representatives a 'brood of vipers' (Matt. 3:7). He warned them not to rely on their nationality for acceptance with God: 'And do not think you can say to yourselves, "We have Abraham as our father." I tell you that out of these stones God can raise up children for Abraham' (v. 9).

The Lord Jesus himself took the same line when faced with opposition from Israel's leaders. They claimed to be Abraham's offspring. 'Abraham is our father,' they asserted (John 8:39); 'The only Father we have is God himself' (v. 41). After showing the incompatibility of such claims with their treatment of him, Jesus said, 'You belong to your father, the devil, and you want to carry out your father's desires' (v. 44).

Zacchaeus, on the contrary, showed himself to be a true 'son of

Abraham' (Luke 19:9) through repentance and faith displayed in his actions. In addition, astonished by the great faith of a Gentile centurion, Jesus said to those following him,

> Truly I tell you, I have not found anyone in Israel with such great faith. I say to you that many will come from the east and the west, and will take their places at the feast with Abraham, Isaac and Jacob in the kingdom of heaven. But the subjects of the kingdom will be thrown outside, into the darkness (Matt. 8:10–12).

Notice, incidentally, that the Jewish patriarchs are in the kingdom of heaven!

Paul the apostle

When we turn to the apostle Paul—a man with an impressive Jewish and religious pedigree—we find him crystal clear about Abraham being 'the father of us all' (Rom. 4:16)—that is, of all who believe, irrespective of nationality. Commenting on Romans 2:28, the *ESV Study Bible* says, 'In striking contrast to the Jewish beliefs of his day, Paul claims that true Jewishness and genuine circumcision are not ethnic or physical matters.'[1]

That claim is supported by what Paul says a little later in 9:6–8, where he argues that 'not all who are descended from Israel are Israel'; and that 'it is not the children by physical descent who are God's children, but it is the children of the promise who are regarded as Abraham's offspring' (see also Rev. 2:9; 3:9).

That is why Paul can, when writing to a predominantly Gentile church, talk about Abraham's people in Old Testament times as being 'our ancestors' (1 Cor. 10:1). He doesn't see Gentile converts as distinct from Jewish ones.

Paul develops this further in his letter to the Galatians. Over against those who want Gentile believers to become Jewish, Paul argues that they are already true 'children of Abraham' (Gal. 3:7), having believed the same gospel God had preached beforehand to Abraham (v. 8). He proclaims the cross of Jesus as the means by which 'the blessing given to Abraham might come to the Gentiles' (v. 14). It is 'in Christ Jesus', he writes, that 'you are all children of God through faith' (v. 26). 'If you belong to Christ, then you are Abraham's seed, and heirs according to the promise' (v. 29).

In case anyone is still unclear as to the identity of the true inheritors of the promise God made to Abraham, Paul draws an allegory from Abraham's two sons—one born by a slave woman and one by a free woman. He portrays the two women as representing two covenants. Hagar represents the Old Covenant made at Sinai, corresponding to the present Jerusalem, 'because she is in slavery with her children' (4:25). Sarah represents the New Covenant and Jerusalem above.

The international believers who made up the churches in Galatia were, like Isaac, the children of promise; this was why they were the objects of Jewish opposition. 'But what does Scripture say? "Get rid of the slave woman and her son, for the slave woman's son will never share in the inheritance with the free woman's son." Therefore, brothers and sisters, we are not children of the slave woman, but of the free woman' (4:30–31).

So who are the inheritors of the promise made to Abraham? Not those who belong to 'the present city of Jerusalem', but those who belong to 'the Jerusalem that is above' (4:25–26). They are 'the Israel of God' (6:16).[2]

With this understanding of how the Old Testament promises find their fulfilment in Christ and his believing people, we are not surprised by New Testament writers using terms for the church that were originally used in the Old Testament of God's people BC. Irrespective of nationality, believers in Christ are the chosen people (Col. 3:12; 1 Peter 2:9), the circumcision (Rom. 3:29; Phil. 3:3), a spiritual house made from living stones (1 Tim. 3:12, 15; Heb. 3:6; 1 Peter 2:5), a holy priesthood (1 Peter

2:5; Rev. 1:6; 5:10), a people for his own possession (Titus 2:14; 1 Peter 2:9) and God's people (Rom. 9:24–26; 1 Peter 2:10).

Through his death the Good Shepherd has brought in his 'other sheep', not of the Jewish fold. His intent in doing so was that there would be 'one flock and one shepherd' (John 10:16; see also 11:49–52). Out of the two historical divisions of Jew and Gentile, Christ has created one new man, neither Jewish nor Gentile. Through the cross, those who were 'foreigners and strangers' are now 'fellow citizens with God's people and also members of his household' (Eph. 2:19). Gentile believers are now 'heirs together' with Jewish believers, 'through the gospel … members together of one body, and sharers together in the promise in Christ Jesus' (3:6). The climax of God's eternal purpose will see the holy city, the heavenly Jerusalem, adorned with the names of the twelve tribes of Israel on its gates, and the names of the twelve apostles[3] of the Lamb on the twelve foundations of its walls (Rev. 21:12–14); one people inhabiting one eternal city.

In a foreword to Alec Motyer's latest book, *A Christian's Pocket Guide to Loving the Old Testament*, Tim Keller recalls being at a seminar where Alec Motyer was questioned about the relationship between Old Testament Israel and the church. Motyer asked his listeners to imagine how the Israelites under Moses would have given their 'testimony' to someone who asked for it. They would have said something like this, he claimed:

We were in a foreign land, in bondage, under the sentence of death. But our mediator— the one who stands between us and God—came to us with the promise of deliverance. We trusted in the promises of God, took shelter under the blood of the Lamb, and he led us out. Now we are on the way to the Promised Land. We are not there yet, of course, but we have the law to guide us, and through blood sacrifice we also have his presence in our midst. So he will stay with us until we get to our true country, our everlasting home.

Motyer then concluded, 'Now think about it. A Christian today could say the same thing, almost word for word.'[4]

'Therefore what God has joined together, let no one separate' (Matt. 19:6).

Chapter 2

NOTES

1 *ESV Study Bible* (Wheaton, IL: Crossway, 2008).

2 Notice that, when in Gal. 4:27 Paul quotes from Isa. 54, he sees it as fulfilled not in a restoration of national and territorial Israel, but in the heavenly people and country. James similarly saw Amos's prophecy about David's tent being rebuilt as being fulfilled in God visiting the Gentiles to take from them 'a people for himself', Acts 15:13–17.

3 'There can be no doubt that the number chosen was deliberate. He [Jesus] saw the twelve apostles as equivalent to the twelve tribes of Israel. He and the apostles together would form the nucleus of a new and purified Israel.' John Stott, *Through the Bible, Through the Year: Daily Reflections from Genesis to Revelation* (Oxford: Lion Hudson, 2006), p. 182.

4 Alec Motyer, *A Christian's Pocket Guide to Loving the Old Testament* (Fearn: Christian Focus, 2015), p. x.

One gospel

How have the one people of God become such? Has there always been one way to God or have there been different routes depending on the time in which people lived and the nation to which they belonged? In short, is there only one gospel, or are there more than one?

Well, there is *the gospel of the kingdom*. That is the message Jesus preached (Matt. 4:23; 24:14; Luke 4:43; 8:1; 16:16), as did Philip in Samaria (Acts 8:12) and Paul at Ephesus (Acts 20:25).

Then there is *the gospel of God*, which was preached by Jesus (Mark 1:14), Paul (Rom. 1:1; 1 Thes. 2:8–9; see also 2 Cor. 4:4; 1 Tim. 1:11) and Peter (1 Peter 4:17).

Paul the apostle refers to what he calls *my gospel* (Rom. 2:16; 16:25; 2 Tim. 2:8) and *our gospel* (2 Cor. 4:3; 1 Thes. 1:5; 2 Thes. 2:14), though without a hint that it originated with 'him' or 'them', nor any desire to detract from it having come from God.

Mark introduces his work as the beginning of *the gospel about Jesus Christ*. This focus on the Lord Jesus is picked up by Stephen (Acts 8:35; 11:20) and Paul (Acts 17:18; Rom. 1:1–3). In a similar vein Paul writes of *the gospel of Christ* (Rom. 15:19; 2 Cor. 2:12; Gal. 1:7; Phil. 1:27; cf. 2 Thes. 1:8).

We also read about *the gospel of God's grace* (Acts 20:24), *the gospel of your salvation* (Eph. 1:13), *the gospel of peace* (Eph. 6:15) and *the eternal gospel* (Rev. 14:6).

And then there are the times when we read about *this gospel*. The Lord Jesus didn't feel the need to define it in Matthew 26:13. Paul referred to it as the gospel by which his readers had been saved (1 Cor. 15:2), and the gospel which unites Jewish and Gentile believers in one body (Eph. 3:6–7).

However, the New Testament writers predominantly refer simply to *the gospel*. Paul saw the need to distinguish it from different gospels which weren't good news at all, but never to distinguish it from other genuine gospels (Gal. 1:6–9). When writing about *the gospel*, Bible writers never anticipate the question 'To which one are you referring?' The implication is that the church has ever known only one gospel.

Interchangeable terms

This is borne out by the fact that descriptions of the one gospel are used interchangeably.

For example, see how Mark introduces Jesus' preaching ministry: 'After John was put in prison, Jesus went into Galilee, proclaiming the good news of God. "The time has come," he said. "The kingdom of God has come near. Repent and believe the good news!"' (1:14–15).

What did Jesus call on his hearers to do? They were to repent and believe the good news. And what was that good news, that gospel? It was 'the good news of God', which was about 'the kingdom of God' having 'come near'.

Another example is to be found in Paul's farewell talk to the elders from the church at Ephesus. Among other things he says to them, '... I consider my life worth nothing to me; my only aim is to finish the race and complete the task the Lord Jesus has given me—the task of testifying to the good news of God's grace. Now I know that none of you among whom I have gone about preaching the kingdom will ever see me again' (Acts 20:24–25).

What was it Paul preached and testified to? In verse 24 it is 'the good news [gospel] of God's grace'. In verse 25 it is 'the kingdom'. The two terms are synonymous. The gospel of the kingdom is the gospel of God's grace. By believing it we are brought under the Kingship of Jesus Christ, becoming his subjects by God's grace alone.

The various ways in which the gospel is mentioned should not be read as titles for different messages from God, but as descriptions of the one message in all its profundity and scope. Here's the great description of it at the beginning of Paul's letter to the Romans:

Paul, a servant of Christ Jesus, called to be an apostle and set apart for the gospel of God—the gospel he promised beforehand through his prophets in the Holy Scriptures regarding his Son, who as to his earthly life was a descendant of David, and who through the Spirit of holiness was appointed the Son of God in power by his resurrection from the dead: Jesus Christ our Lord (1:1–4).

Old Testament gospel

In the circles I grew up in, it was thought that the Old Testament was a book of law and the New Testament a book of grace. Some drew an even sharper line, thinking the Synoptic Gospels were not as much based on grace as are the letters of Paul. Dr Scofield even claimed that what we call the Sermon on the Mount is 'pure law', finding its basis of forgiveness as 'legal ground' (Matt. 6:12), as distinct from Ephesians 4:32, 'which is grace'.[1]

If he was right, forgiveness pre-Pentecost was down to what a person deserved, while afterwards it was unmerited. But the whole New Testament protests at such an idea.

The letter to the Romans is a great exposition of justification by grace alone, through faith alone, in Christ alone, and it argues that such has always been the way people have been saved from God's just judgement. The writer sees the problem back in Old Testament times not of God being judgemental, but of him seeming to have been far too lenient. '[I]n his forbearance [God] had left the sins committed beforehand unpunished' (Rom. 3:25), which raised questions about his righteousness. How could God clear his name when he was so soft on sin and sinners? Only in the gospel is God's righteousness vindicated.

Peter's address in the home of Cornelius is interesting in this regard. There he sees the apostolic message in terms of warning about judgement to come, whereas the Old Testament prophets brought a message of forgiveness. Here are his words: '[Jesus] commanded us to preach to the people and to testify that he is the one whom God appointed as judge of the living and the dead. All the prophets testify about him that everyone who believes in him receives forgiveness of sins through his name' (Acts 10:42–43). Peter was commanded by Christ to testify that Jesus is the God-appointed Judge; the ancient prophets, that forgiveness is available to everyone who believes in him. The Old Testament is a book of grace as much as the New Testament.

Paul the apostle draws two famous examples of this in Romans 4. The first is Abraham, the father of the faithful. Paul wants to know whether he was put right with God on the basis of what he deserved or not. Was it the good works he came up with that put him right in God's sight, or was it his simple faith in the promise of God? He concludes that it wasn't Abraham's achievements that he was rewarded for, but his trust in God his Saviour (Rom. 4:1–3).

Nor was it his nationality that gave him a head start. Someone, referring to Abraham, once observed that the first Jew was a Gentile. He was acquitted by God of his guilt before he was circumcised (Rom. 4:9–12), and long before God gave his law to Moses (4:13–15).

King David is another case in point. Paul quotes Psalm 32 to demonstrate that Israel's famous king was also made right with God on the basis of grace, not works (Rom. 4:6–8).

And we could trawl through the lives of other Old Testament believers to show the same thing. We can even go back as far as Noah. Why did God save him from the deluge he brought on the earth? Here's the Bible's own explanation: 'Noah found favour [grace] in the eyes of the LORD' (Gen. 6:8). Or, as Alec Motyer loves to explain it, 'Grace found Noah.'[2]

Now, of course, though we are saved by grace alone, the grace that saves doesn't come alone. And so we aren't surprised to learn, in the next verse, that 'Noah was a righteous man, blameless among the people of his time, and he walked faithfully with God' (6:9). But that's what God's grace made him, not what Noah was before grace took hold of him.

We could also take note of Job—a man so exceptionally 'righteous' that God pointed him out to Satan as Exhibit A when it came to loyalty to God and holy living; and yet the book draws to a close with the great man saying, 'I despise myself and repent in dust and ashes' (Job 42:6). His hope lay not in himself, but in his Redeemer (19:25).

Chapter 3

NOTES

1 *The Scofield Reference Bible* (Oxford: Oxford University Press, 1917)
2 Alec Motyer, *Discovering the Old Testament* (Leicester: Crossway, 2006), p. 63.

One kingdom

We have already touched on the subject of the kingdom of God in Chapter 3, but it is time to ask whether there are two kingdoms: one territorial and the other spiritual.

How does what we call 'The New Testament' begin? What are Matthew's first words? Here they are: 'This is the genealogy of Jesus the Messiah the son of David, the son of Abraham …'

The striking thing about that statement is that David lived centuries after Abraham and yet he is mentioned first here. In fact, in this list of Jesus' ancestors, David is the key figure. And when the angel turns up to tell Joseph that his wife-to-be is going to give birth to a son, he addresses Jesus' stepfather as 'Joseph son of David' (Matt. 1:20; Luke records the angel telling Mary that her firstborn son would be given 'the throne of his father David', 1:32).

When various people came to Jesus, imploring him to intervene miraculously on their behalf, Matthew records them as addressing him as 'Son of David' (Matt. 9:27; 15:22; 20:30–31). People were astonished by Jesus' ability to perform miraculous cures and asked, 'Could this be the Son of David?' (12:23). When Jesus rode into Jerusalem on a donkey, the crowds shouted, 'Hosanna to the Son of David!' (21:9). And the children said the same in the temple courts (21:15).

But the question arises as to how the Lord Jesus thought of himself in that role. Did he see his mission at the time as being to claim David's kingdom for his own, by ousting the foreign oppressor? Had he come to establish his throne over the nation of Israel? The answer has to be 'No'. When the people came to 'make him king by force, [he] withdrew again to a mountain by himself' (John 6:15). And when Pilate raised the issue of Jesus being 'the king of the Jews', Jesus' response was to say, 'My kingdom is not of this world. If it were, my servants would fight to prevent my arrest by the Jewish leaders. But now my kingdom is from another place' (John 18:36).

Far from coming to liberate his fellow-countrymen from the Roman yoke, Jesus encouraged the Jews to pay the poll-tax levied by the Romans (Matt. 22:15–21). Caesar had no need to fear that this king might raise an army to rise up against the empire. King Jesus was not interested in gaining territory to rule over or in liberating his people from their invaders. His objectives were far different.

Before we probe those aims and intentions, let's backtrack more than five centuries to the time when world dominion was no longer in the hands of Jewish kings. Daniel is in Babylon, where he outlines to its king the divinely foretold course of world history. It reaches a climax when, in the days of certain kings, 'the God of heaven will set up a kingdom that will never be destroyed' (Dan. 2:44). On releasing Daniel from a den of lions, King Darius said of Daniel's God, 'For he is the living God and he endures for ever; his kingdom will not be destroyed, his dominion will never end' (6:26).

In the next chapter Daniel is given a vision of one 'like a son of man, coming with the clouds of heaven' (7:13). And this is what Daniel saw happen to this person: 'He was given authority, glory and sovereign power; all nations and peoples of every language worshipped him. His dominion is an everlasting dominion that will not pass away, and his kingdom is one that will never be destroyed … His kingdom will be an everlasting kingdom, and all rulers will worship and obey him' (7:14, 27).

This is the event to which all prophecy ultimately points, and it was what believers in Israel were looking for when Christ appeared (see Luke 1:67–70; 2:38; 23:51). Disappointment set in among some when Jesus, instead of overthrowing the aggressors and establishing his kingdom, ended up on a cross. '[W]e had hoped that he was the one who was going to redeem Israel,' they said with disappointment (Luke 24:21). And it was still on the minds of the disciples after Jesus rose from the dead (Acts 1:6).

The kingdom has come

ITS FIRST PREACHER

The first preacher of the kingdom was a man called John. He drew vast crowds from their normal occupations out into the desert to hear the good news he was proclaiming. Matthew sums up John's message in these words: 'Repent, for the kingdom of heaven has come near' (Matt. 3:2). The kingdom of heaven had drawn near because the King of heaven had arrived on a state visit, John being his ambassador and herald.

But how should the people prepare for the visit of their King? Should they raise an army to fight for his cause? Should they build him a palace to occupy? How should they show their allegiance to him?

Their preparation is summed up in a single-word demand. John called on the people to 'repent', and to demonstrate it by being baptized. To repent is to have a change of mind. In this case it means a change of mind regarding God and his rights and demands. Such repentance is an indispensable term of entry into God's kingdom; for rebellion against a sovereign of necessity excludes a person from his kingdom.

Alongside repentance comes faith. Paul was later to sum up John's message in these words: 'John's baptism was a baptism of repentance. He told the people to believe in the one coming after him, that is, in Jesus' (Acts 19:4). The genuineness of such belief in Jesus would be seen in changed lives (Matt. 3:8).

ITS SUPREME PREACHER

The Lord Jesus began his preaching ministry using the same words as John the Baptist: 'After John was put in prison, Jesus went into Galilee, proclaiming the good news of God. "The time has come," he said. "The

kingdom of God has come near. Repent and believe the good news!"'
(Mark 1:14–15). The time had not come for Jesus to come with the clouds
of heaven, but rather to prepare the way whereby sinful humans could
find a place in the kingdom yet to come.

John the apostle gives us an example of Jesus proclaiming the kingdom
privately to Nicodemus, a member of the Jewish council. He laid out the
terms of entrance into the kingdom twice over: 'Very truly I tell you, no
one can see the kingdom of God unless they are born again' (John 3:3);
'Very truly I tell you, no one can enter the kingdom of God unless they are
born of water and the Spirit' (3:5).

Earlier John had used new birth terminology to describe the essential
requirement for a place in the family of God: '... to all who did receive
him, to those who believed in his name, he gave the right to become
children of God—children born not of natural descent, nor of human
decision or a husband's will, but born of God' (1:12–13). To Nicodemus
it was a prerequisite for entrance into God's kingdom, whether in its
present or its future form. The idea of being born again is also found in
the writings of Paul, Peter and John (Titus 3:5; 1 Peter 1:3, 23; 1 John
2:29; 3:9; 4:7; 5:1, 4, 18).

The arrival of God's kingdom with the coming of Jesus was not the
kingdom in its ultimate manifestation. Asked by the Pharisees when that
kingdom would come, Jesus replied, 'The coming of the kingdom of God
is not something that can be observed, nor will people say, "Here it is," or
"There it is," because the kingdom of God is in your midst' (Luke
17:20–21).

At Nazareth on one occasion, Jesus described his mission in terms of
what Isaiah had written at 61:1–2. What is fascinating is that he rolled up
the scroll and returned it to the attendant before completing the quotation
(Luke 4:18–19). He stopped mid-sentence before the words 'and the day
of vengeance of our God'. The previous predictions he fulfilled that day,
but not the one that still awaits the Last Day.

So the kingdom had come, but not in its final form. The works of Jesus were a sign that, in one sense, the kingdom of God had come, but, in another, the full life of the kingdom waited another day. The blind seeing, the lame walking, people being cured of their leprosy, the deaf being able to hear again and the dead being raised: this was all evidence that Jesus is the King over God's kingdom and that, when he comes in glory, all those sad aspects that mark 'the old order of things' will be no more.

Currently, the kingdom grows by the sowing of good seed (Matt. 13:1–3). It will yet be seen visibly and fully at the time that Jesus calls the 'harvest' (Matt. 13:24–30, 36–43). As did John, so the Lord Jesus spoke of the need for repentance and faith, expressed in baptism, as the terms of entrance into the kingdom. And he taught that changed lives would prove the reality of those things (Matt. 7:16–19).

ITS APOSTOLIC PREACHER

When we turn to Paul, we find that he too talks about the kingdom of God. Speaking to the elders of the church at Ephesus, Paul summed up his work among them as 'preaching the kingdom' (Acts 20:25). And when Luke reports on Paul's two years in Rome under house arrest, he says, 'He proclaimed the kingdom of God and taught about the Lord Jesus Christ—with all boldness and without hindrance!' (Acts 28:31). He taught the Romans that 'the kingdom of God is not a matter of eating and drinking, but of righteousness, peace and joy in the Holy Spirit' (Rom. 14:17). He reminded the Colossians that God has 'rescued us from the dominion of darkness and brought us into the kingdom of the Son he loves, in whom we have redemption, the forgiveness of sins' (Col. 1:13–14).

And what did Paul teach both Jews and Gentiles as the way into the kingdom? He told them that they must 'turn to God in repentance and have faith in our Lord Jesus' (Acts 20:21). How would the reality of such 'repentance and faith' be seen? In changed lives (Acts 26:20).

The coming of our Lord Jesus to our world was Stage One of the coming kingdom of God. In its current form the kingdom is established in the hearts of human beings who turn to God in repentance and put their faith in the Lord Jesus. It is solely a spiritual matter.

The kingdom has not yet come

However, though we can think of the kingdom as having come with the first coming of Jesus, its universal and eternal reality has yet to come. The Lord Jesus encouraged his followers to pray, 'your kingdom come' (Matt. 6:10). We don't ask for something we already have! The criminal crucified next to Jesus asked to be remembered 'when you come into your kingdom' (Luke 23:42). Christ himself spoke of the great divide which the coming kingdom will bring about: 'I say to you that many will come from the east and the west, and will take their places at the feast with Abraham, Isaac and Jacob in the kingdom of heaven. But the subjects of the kingdom will be thrown outside, into the darkness, where there will be weeping and gnashing of teeth' (Matt. 8:11–12; for the same reality described in parabolic form, see Matt. 13:36–43, 47–50).

Paul charged Timothy with preaching the word 'in view of [Christ's] appearing and his kingdom' (2 Tim. 4:1). He himself looked forward to the Lord bringing him to 'his heavenly kingdom' (4:18). Peter shows his readers how to 'receive a rich welcome into the eternal kingdom of our Lord and Saviour Jesus Christ' (2 Peter 1:11).

All those grand prophecies throughout the Old Testament about the universal and eternal kingdom of God and of Christ will reach their fulfilment one day, often in ways beyond what the original writers understood. At its due time, the phenomenal moment will arrive to which John refers when he says, 'Then I heard every creature in heaven and on earth and under the earth and on the sea, and all that is in them, singing: "To him who sits on the throne and to the Lamb be praise and honour and glory and power, for ever and ever!"' (Rev. 5:13). Loud voices in heaven will yet exclaim, 'The kingdom of the world has become the kingdom of our Lord and of his Messiah, and he will reign for ever and ever' (Rev. 11:15).

Well might we sing the words,

Oh that, with yonder sacred throng,
We at his feet may fall,
Join in the everlasting song
And crown him Lord of all!
(Edward Perronet, 1780)

One hope

'The God of glory appeared to our father Abraham while he was still in Mesopotamia, before he lived in Haran. "Leave your country and your people," God said, "and go to the land I will show you"' (Acts 7:2–3). That's how Stephen started his reply to the high priest as he stood before the Sanhedrin, a body of men he later described as 'stiff-necked … [with] hearts and ears … still uncircumcised … [who] always resist the Holy Spirit!' (Acts 7:51).

The Promised Land

Yes, in addition to God promising to make Abram into a great nation and the means of blessing to 'all peoples on earth', God promised territory for him and his descendants to inherit (Gen. 12:1–3). Their homeland would be called 'Canaan' (12:5). Its area is variously described in Scripture.

Abraham was told that the Promised Land would stretch 'from the Wadi of Egypt to the great river, the Euphrates' (Gen. 15:18). Moses was promised that Israel's borders would stretch 'from the Red Sea to the Mediterranean Sea, and from the desert to the Euphrates River' (Exod. 23:31). Joshua was told, 'Your territory will extend from the desert to Lebanon, and from the great river, the Euphrates—all the Hittite country—to the Mediterranean Sea in the west' (Josh. 1:4).

Interestingly, in the four thousand years since God made the promise to Abram, the only time Israel's boundaries ever approached these limits was probably during the reign of King Solomon (1 Kings 4:21–25; 2 Chr. 9:26). This is indeed curious as more than once the promise was that the land would belong to Abram's descendants as 'an everlasting possession' (Gen. 17:8; 48:4). They would not actually have possession of the land as owners, but as tenants, 'as foreigners and strangers' (Lev. 25:23).

Before they ever entered the land of promise, the people were frequently warned that they would forfeit the land if they became rebellious (see, e.g., Lev. 18:28; 20:22; 26:33, 38–39; Deut. 4:25–26; 28:36–37, 64–68). Later, when the Lord appeared to King Solomon, he repeated the warning (1 Kings 9:6–7). And because Israel refused to listen to the warnings, the Assyrians came and took them into exile (2 Kings 17:5–8), followed later by the carrying away of Judah to Babylon (2 Kings 25:11, 21; cf. Jer. 9:13–16).

The Lord had also promised that, if his people turned back to him, he would bring them back from the lands where he had scattered them (Deut. 30:1–5; Jer. 24:4–7; 29:10–14; Ezek. 11:14–17). In line with his word, a remnant of Judah returned in 'the first year of Cyrus king of Persia' under the leadership of Ezra the scribe (Ezra 1:1–3). The Major Prophets wrote enthusiastically of this great restoration of the land (e.g. Isa. 35; Ezek. 36–37). And yet Ezra had to warn the pilgrims who returned that they would only be able to 'leave [the land] to your children as an everlasting inheritance' (Ezra 9:12) if they remained loyal to the Lord and obeyed his word.

We are not surprised to discover that things degenerated following the return from exile, and that Zechariah had to look forward to yet another return from exile 'from the countries of the east and the west' (Zech. 8:7). He linked it with the day of the LORD, the day when 'The LORD will be king over the whole earth. On that day there will be one LORD, and his name the only name' (Zech. 14:9). Isaiah speaks of it as the day when the LORD 'will create new heavens and a new earth' (Isa. 65:17; 66:22).

When will these promises be fulfilled, and how will they be fulfilled? To find out, we have to wait for the coming of the Person in whom all God's promises find their fulfilment. He and his personally appointed representatives will tell us when and how.

A redirected promise

One of the striking features of the New Testament is its lack of concern for, and interest in, the land of promise. This is even more fascinating because it opens with the land under occupation by a foreign power, and spans the time when Jerusalem and its temple were destroyed in AD 70 by Emperor Titus. Yet none of these circumstances call, from Christ or his apostles, any promise of the overthrow of the Romans and the recovery of the land.

Though the Lord Jesus lived in 'the land' while it was under enemy occupation, he never raised the issue—apart from requiring the payment of taxes to the invaders—and, post-Pentecost, his followers never mentioned it.

For the vision had broadened out. The meek would not now inherit the *land*, but the *earth* (compare Ps. 37:11 with Matt. 5:5). Abraham is not now the inheritor of the land of Canaan, but the 'heir of the world' (Rom. 4:13). The promise is now seen to be fulfilled in Abraham and his spiritual descendants in the world to come.

The writer of the letter to the Hebrews points out that Abraham was content to camp down in Canaan 'like a stranger in a foreign country … [living] in tents' because 'he was looking forward to the city with foundations, whose architect and builder is God' (Heb. 11:9–10). His eyes were on something much greater than Canaan. Nor was he alone in so doing. The true children of Abraham lived 'admitting that they were foreigners and strangers on earth … [and] were longing for a better country—a heavenly one' (11:13, 16). In fact, as the writer concludes his biographical snippets of the Old Testament people of faith, he says this about them, including those who lived in the land of promise: 'These were all commended for their faith, yet none of them received what had been promised' (11:39).

They were all living by faith when they died, even though many of them were living in Canaan. Why? Because they saw the promise as something far greater than inhabiting a small piece of real estate on the eastern Mediterranean seaboard.

The Old Testament writer of Psalm 119 says, 'I am a stranger on earth' (Ps. 119:19). King David himself shared that perspective. He prayed this prayer: 'We are foreigners and strangers in your sight, as were all our ancestors. Our days on earth are like a shadow, without hope' (1 Chr. 29:15; cf. Ps. 39:12). They knew that the real inheritance lay on the other side of death, and would be theirs together with the New Testament people of faith; for all who belong to Christ are Abraham's seed 'and heirs according to the promise' (Gal. 3:29). Canaan should have been the land of rest for Israel (Josh. 1:13, 15), but Joshua didn't give the people rest. That's why David spoke of another day of rest in Psalm 95:11 (as quoted in Heb. 4:3): the Sabbath-rest remaining for the people of God (Heb. 4:8–9).

One of the words frequently associated in Old Testament times with the Promised Land was 'inheritance'. God would give them the land 'as an inheritance' (see, e.g., Deut. 4:21, 38; 12:10; 15:4; 19:3; 20:16; 21:23; 24:4; 25:19; 26:1). But when we come to the New Testament letters we find that the word is no longer used of Canaan. The inheritance is now eternal (Heb. 9:15), one from which national Israel is excluded (Gal. 4:21–31). Peter describes it as 'an inheritance that can never perish, spoil or fade ... kept in heaven for you ...' (1 Peter 1:4).

What a glorious inheritance awaits the child of God! Well did Isaac Watts pen the words

O could we make our doubts remove,
Those gloomy thoughts that rise,
And see the Canaan that we love
With unbeclouded eyes!

Could we but climb where Moses stood
And view the landscape o'er,

Not Jordan's stream, nor death's cold flood,

Should fright us from the shore.

('There Is a Land of Pure Delight', 1707)

A heavenly city

If Old Testament Canaan was a pledge of a better country to come, earthly Jerusalem was also the pledge of the heavenly city for which Old Testament pilgrims longed.

The Old Testament places a great emphasis on Israel's capital city in Canaan. It was where the LORD placed his name, the place to which the tribes would come at festival times. We therefore receive a profound shock as we listen in on a conversation between Jesus and a woman at Sychar's well. Possibly to divert the conversation from the uncomfortable direction it was taking, she raises a thorny issue between Jews and Samaritans. Where is the right place to worship God: Gerizim or Jerusalem? Surely Jesus will jump to the defence of Jerusalem, won't he? But he doesn't. This is what he says: 'Woman ... believe me, a time is coming when you will worship the Father neither on this mountain nor in Jerusalem' (John 4:21). The days when location was important for worship were rapidly coming to an end. Jerusalem and its temple were about to be rendered obsolete in that regard.

In a striking analogy drawn from Sarah and Hagar, Paul says that 'the present city of Jerusalem ... is in slavery with her children' (Gal. 4:25). It will never be anything different from that. If it's freedom you want, you need to look to 'the Jerusalem that is above', the mother of all believers (4:26). In fact, the writer of Hebrews sees his readers as having already 'come to Mount Zion, to the city of the living God, the heavenly Jerusalem' (Heb. 12:22). The city of God (Rev. 3:12) and the holy city are now the new Jerusalem 'coming down out of heaven from God' (Rev. 21:2, 10). And the people of God—Old Testament and New Testament—inhabit the eternal city as one people (Rev. 21:12, 14).

Chapter 5

Saviour, if of Zion's city
I through grace a member am,
Let the world deride or pity,
I will glory in your name;
Fading is the worldling's pleasure,
All his boasted pomp and show;
Solid joys and lasting treasure
None but Zion's children know.
(John Newton, 'Glorious Things of Thee Are Spoken', 1779)

There is, however, one important omission from the heavenly Jerusalem. 'I did not see a temple in the city,' John affirms, 'because the Lord God Almighty and the Lamb are its temple' (Rev. 21:22). Herod's temple will not be rebuilt. The earthly sanctuary was, after all, simply 'a copy and shadow of what is in heaven' (Heb. 8:5). It has been rendered obsolete by a greater temple, the Christ himself, the one and only true meeting place between us and God (John 2:18–22).

The Bible is again seen to be one book. It speaks about one people of Abraham and one inheritance. The difference between the two volumes is simply that of promise and fulfilment; but the fulfilment always outshines the old expectations. The earthly inheritance was a shadow of the heavenly, the earthly city was a shadow of the heavenly, and the earthly temple was a shadow of the heavenly.

When Paul arrived in Rome as a prisoner, he called together the local Jewish leaders and said to them, 'It is because of the hope of Israel that I am bound with this chain' (Acts 28:20). It ought to be obvious what he didn't mean by that. He wasn't saying that he had been going around preaching Jewish superiority over Gentiles, or a kingdom over which Israel would be chief among the nations. If he had, he wouldn't have arrived in Rome in chains. He would rather have been applauded by his accusers.

No; the Jews had arrested Paul on the charge that he 'teaches everyone everywhere against our people and our law and this place [the temple]' (Acts 21:28). What angered them was that Paul claimed to have been sent 'far away to the Gentiles' (22:21). What aroused their animosity was that Paul saw the hope of Israel as being, at the same time, the hope of the nations; that 'the promise our twelve tribes are hoping to see fulfilled' (26:6–8) was fulfilled in Christ raised from the dead.

For Jesus of Nazareth is indeed the Saviour of the world. God announced the gospel to Abraham in these words: 'All nations will be blessed through you' (Gal. 3:8). And it is in the good news of Jesus Christ that the ancient hopes are realized to Jew and Gentile equally.

We know that the whole creation has been groaning as in the pains of childbirth right up to the present time. Not only so, but we ourselves, who have the firstfruits of the Spirit, groan inwardly as we wait eagerly for our adoption to sonship, the redemption of our bodies. For in this hope we [both Jew and Gentile] were saved. But hope that is seen is no hope at all. Who hopes for what they already have? But if we hope for what we do not yet have, we wait for it patiently (Rom. 8:22–25).

The Israel of God

A book like this would be incomplete if it did not address Romans 9–11, chapters in which Paul struggles with the fortunes of his fellow-countrymen, the Jews.

Sadly, these chapters have at times been treated as though they don't belong to the rest of the letter. They are too often read as though they have nothing to do with the preceding and succeeding chapters. And yet the position of Jews and Gentiles, as they relate to God and to one another through the gospel of Christ, is never far below the surface throughout this letter.

In 1:16 Paul has affirmed that the gospel 'is the power of God that brings salvation to everyone who believes: first to the Jew, then to the Gentile'. '[S]alvation is from the Jews' (John 4:22). That's where it began, for Christ was physically descended from Abraham. The proclaiming of repentance and faith to all nations would begin in Jerusalem (Luke 24:47). It was from that location that Christ's witnesses would travel 'in all Judea and Samaria, and to the ends of the earth' (Acts 1:8). From Jerusalem the gospel would go out into all the world (Matt. 28:19). Jerusalem was the beginning; the whole world was the goal.

In Romans 2:17–29 Paul addresses those who call themselves Jews because of their physical ancestry; he explains that a Jew in God's sight is not someone who has had a certain physical operation or has come from one particular people group, but someone (of whatever nationality) who has experienced an internal transformation by the Spirit of God.

Yes, the Jews had been singularly privileged, as Paul points out in chapter 3. But he then proceeds to show that, before God, Jews and Gentiles are alike. 'What shall we conclude then? Do we [Jews] have any advantage? Not at all! For we have already made the charge that Jews and Gentiles alike are all under the power of sin' (3:9). He continues, 'There is no difference between Jew and Gentile, for all have sinned and fall short of the glory of God, and all are justified freely by his grace through the redemption that came by Christ Jesus' (3:22–24; compare v. 22 with 10:12).

Furthermore, towards the end of chapter 3 he asks, 'Is God the God of Jews only? Is he not the God of Gentiles too? Yes, of Gentiles too, since there is only one God, who will justify the circumcised by faith and the uncircumcised through that same faith' (vv. 29–30). We all come to God the same way—by grace alone, through faith alone, in Christ alone.

The problem Paul encountered in his evangelistic endeavours was that, while the Gentiles were often open and receptive, his fellow-countrymen were largely antagonistic to his message and persecuted the messengers. It became so bad that Paul said his Jewish adversaries 'killed the Lord Jesus and the prophets and also drove us out. They displease God and are hostile to everyone in their effort to keep us from speaking to the Gentiles so that they may be saved. In this way they always heap up their sins to the limit. The wrath of God has come upon them at last' (1 Thes. 2:15–16).

This is what seems to be on Paul's mind as we reach chapter 9 of Romans. Has God in his wrath excluded the Jews from his salvation in Christ? Paul would rather personally be 'cursed and cut off from Christ' (9:3) than see his own kith and kin experience that horror. And so Paul addresses certain issues raised in his mind by Jewish intransigence.

1. Can God be trusted? (9:6–13)

The first question he raises has to do with all those Old Testament promises God made to bless the people of Israel. Have they gone up in smoke? Paul's response is that you have to work out who 'Israel' really is. He's already made the point in 2:28–29, but he develops the theme further here: 'For not all who are descended from Israel are Israel,' he says in verse 6. 'Nor because they are his descendants are they all Abraham's children,' he notes in verse 7 (for the true children of Abraham, see Gal. 3:29). His point is that we aren't God's children on account of our physical pedigree. Such seeming advantages of nationality and ancestry can easily become obstacles rather than helps to our becoming God's children (Phil. 3:7).

Paul illustrates his point from Ishmael and Isaac. The children of the promise came from the supernaturally born Isaac, not through the naturally born Ishmael (Gen. 18:10, 14). Similarly, God sovereignly chose Jacob, not Esau, though both were sons of Isaac (Gen. 25:23; Mal. 1:2–3). And that's how it always is (John 1:11–13). God hasn't failed to keep his word. You simply have to remember what is meant by 'Israel'.

2. Isn't that unfair? (9:14–18)

Is it fair of God to act in this way, choosing some people and not others? It might be unfair if justice is the overriding consideration. But which of us can afford justice from God? Not one! All we can appeal to God for is mercy, and thank God that our salvation does not 'depend on human desire or effort, but on God's mercy' (v. 16).

3. Isn't it unreasonable? (9:19–29)

Paul throws a third question into the arena. How can God blame us for being hopeless cases if that is what we are? If he makes the decisions, why does he blame us for the results of them?

The chapter responds in two ways. The first is to point out that God's sovereign prerogative is similar to that of a potter with a lump of clay (vv. 20–21). So, though it is permissible to question God, it is arrogantly futile to quarrel with him. The second point is that God's gracious intent is predominantly the salvation of those to whom he shows mercy.

He backs this up with a couple of Old Testament references. To address the amazing inclusion of the Gentiles in God's salvation he goes back to the prophet Hosea, who says, 'I will say to those called "Not my

people", "You are my people"; and they will say, "You are my God."'
And again, '… they will be called "children of the living God"' (Hosea
2:23; 1:10; cf. 1 Peter 2:10).

Then, in verses 27–29 Paul homes in on Isaiah 10:22–23 and 1:9 to show
that, in spite of God's promise to make the nation of Israel as numerous as
the sand on the seashore, 'only the remnant will be saved' (v. 27). Paul
wasn't shocked by unbelieving Israel; it had been foretold.

The true people of God, this chapter proclaims, are not limited to
Abraham's physical descendants. Far from it! They will include those
who previously were far off but have been brought near by the blood of
Christ; people formerly 'excluded from citizenship in Israel and
foreigners to the covenants of the promise, without hope and without
God in the world' (Eph. 2:12). Again, we need to remember who makes
up the true Israel, and how these people are formed into one new entity in
Christ. That's where we head next in Romans 9:30 through to 10:21.

4. Two ways to God? (9:30–33)

How does a person find a welcome from God? These verses describe two
ways of seeking God's favour. One is to produce a 'righteousness'
sufficient to win God over. The other is to recognize that such a thing is a
sheer impossibility. Thus the only way into a position of favour with God
is to accept a 'righteousness' provided by him alone (see Phil. 3:1–14,
where Paul works this out in his own experience).

The Gentiles knew they couldn't keep God's holy law, so gratefully
accepted mercy from God and the gift of righteousness through Jesus
Christ. The Jews thought that God had given them the law as a way of
earning his favour and so refused charity, even from God. Was that a
shock to Paul? No. He had read Isaiah 8:14 and 28:16.

5. Why does the wrong way fail? (10:1–4)

Chapter 10 opens with Paul's longing that his fellow-countrymen might be saved. That's the issue throughout these chapters—salvation from the wrath of God, not national supremacy.

In verse 2 we find that sincerity itself doesn't save us; nor (v. 3) does personal effort. Christ alone can save us. He has met all the requirements of God's law on our behalf, and, through the cross, has brought all believers in him to a place where God accepts them as righteous.

6. Why does the right way succeed? (10:5–21)

So how is a person 'saved'? What is the message of faith in Christ over against personal law-keeping? It's in verses 9–10: 'if you declare with your mouth, "Jesus is Lord," and believe in your heart that God raised him from the dead, you will be *saved*. For it is with your heart that you believe and are justified, and it is with your mouth that you profess your faith and are *saved*.'[1]

This message is for all, Jew and Gentile alike: 'For there is no difference between Jew and Gentile—the same Lord is Lord of all and richly blesses all who call on him, for, "Everyone who calls on the name of the Lord will be *saved*"' (vv. 12–13).

The right way succeeds because it depends on Christ and his achievements, not on me and my futile attempts to earn God's favour. So this message must be proclaimed (vv. 14–15), and it must be received (vv. 16–21). The problem for Paul was that the message had been proclaimed to his fellow-countrymen. They had heard it (v. 18); but they didn't truly understand it (vv. 19–20), nor did they repent and believe the gospel, even though, as God puts it, 'All day long I have held out my hands to a disobedient and obstinate people' (v. 21).

The question that raises is this: Has God's patience run out with the Jews? Has he decided 'enough is enough'? Have the Jews put themselves beyond the reach of God's mercy? Is the gospel no longer for them? Is the good news of Jesus Christ only for Gentiles now? We turn to chapter 11.

7. Are Jews excluded? (11:1–10)

'I ask then: did God reject his people?' That's the burning question with which chapter 11 begins. For Paul, the answer had to be a resounding 'NO' because he was of Jewish stock and he had been saved by God through the gospel. He was Exhibit A when it came to God saving Jews from the wrath to come. If the gospel promise had proved true for him (not only a Jew but a previously hostile one, 1 Tim. 1:13, 15–16), clearly Jews were not excluded from the grace of God in Christ.

In Israel's most apostate days, God had not been without a people who were truly his own. Paul quotes from 1 Kings 19:10, 14, 18 to show that, though the prophet Elijah thought he was the only person left in Israel who was loyal to the Lord, there were no fewer than 'seven thousand who have not bowed the knee to Baal'. Similarly, Paul was sure that, in his time, there was also 'a remnant chosen by grace' (v. 5): Jews saved by grace alone, through faith alone, in Christ alone. And it might be a much larger remnant than appeared at first sight.

However, alongside that encouraging truth comes the sober warning of verses 7–10. There continues to be an intransigent majority hardened by God, a people who demand that God will accept them either on merit or not at all. Is this a surprise? Not at all! It was all written about in the Law, the Prophets and the Psalms (Paul quotes from Deut. 29:4; Isa. 29:10; Ps. 69:22–23). Clearly, as he has already affirmed in 9:6, 'not all who are descended from Israel are Israel'.

8. Are Jews beyond recovery? (11:11–32)

But does this 'hardening' by God mean that Jews are now beyond the reach of the gospel? No. The 'hardening' is not God's last word. In fact, two positive things flow from Israel's 'stumbling'. First, God's grace has gone out to the rest of the world. As some Jews are stirred by this, they will turn back to the Lord (vv. 11–16). If grace reaching the Gentiles is a marvel, the subsequent return of grace to many Jews will be even more amazing.

So non-Jews must not be proud or arrogant concerning Israel's 'hardening', as though they are in some way superior to their unbelieving Jewish neighbours. Non-Jewish believers are like cuttings from a wild olive tree being grafted into the cultivated olive tree of Jewish believers (see Eph. 2:11–22 for a different analogy). If unbelieving Jewish branches were cut off to make room for Gentile branches, there is no place for Gentile feelings of superiority. Both Jewish and Gentile branches remain part of the olive tree by faith alone. If God has cut off unbelieving Jewish branches, he is able to do likewise with unbelieving Gentile branches (vv. 16–22). More than that, if unbelieving Jewish branches desist from their unbelief, God is able to graft them in again (vv. 23–24).

In fact, this is what God will do. Israel's present experience of 'hardening' is a temporary arrangement. It will exist 'until the full number of the Gentiles has come in, and in this way all Israel will be saved' (vv. 25–26). And what does it mean to 'be saved'? It means to be saved from God's wrath through faith in Christ alone, irrespective of nationality or personal performance.

Just as there was a 'full inclusion' of Jewish believers back in verse 12, so there will be a 'full number' of God's elect brought in from the nations (v. 25). In this way—by the bringing in of God's elect from the Jewish nation and from the Gentile nations—'all Israel will be saved'. The 'Israel of God' (Gal. 6:16), 'the [true] circumcision' (Phil. 3:3), the 'one flock' (John 10:16), the 'one new humanity' (Eph. 2:15), will be complete.

There are not two ways by which we humans are reconciled to God. It has always been by grace alone. That's what the patriarchs found. Elect Jews are loved and saved by God 'on account of the patriarchs' (Rom. 11:28): Abraham, who believed God's promise; Isaac, the child of the promise (9:8); and Jacob, the chosen son (9:11–13).

Jews and Gentiles alike can only appeal to God for mercy, 'for all have sinned and fall short of the glory of God' (3:23). Pedigree and performance are 'out' when it comes to being 'saved'. It is through the gospel of Christ that God keeps his covenant with the patriarchs.

And so Paul concludes his great panorama of God's plan of salvation which has taken him 11 chapters to complete. And he can only do so with a doxology:

Oh, the depth of the riches of the wisdom and knowledge of God!
How unsearchable his judgements,
and his paths beyond tracing out!
'Who has known the mind of the Lord?
Or who has been his counsellor?'
'Who has ever given to God,
that God should repay him?'
For from him and through him and to him are all things.
To him be the glory for ever! Amen.

NOTES

1 My italics as a reminder that 'salvation' is the issue being addressed in these chapters.

The 'for ever' promises

Does God keep his promises? Is his word to be trusted? I ask these questions because, in the Old Testament, God makes certain promises which include the words 'for ever' and yet they refer to things which haven't lasted 'for ever'. For the purposes of this book we need to look briefly at four of them.

The problem

1. THE LAND

Some people claim that the land of Canaan belongs to the nation of Israel in perpetuity—that God has given them a piece of territory for all time. This claim is made on the basis of God's promise to Abram in Genesis 13:15. There, after Lot had pitched his tent towards Sodom, the Lord appeared to Abram and said, 'All the land that you see I will give to you and your offspring *for ever*.' The extent of the territory 'given' is set out in Genesis 15:18–21 and Numbers 34:1–12.

Our problem is that Israel only ever enjoyed full possession of that Promised Land for a few decades during the reign of King Solomon. So what has happened to the 'for ever' promise?

2. THE MONARCHY

A similar problem arises with the promise of an unending monarchy, though those claiming that the first promise gave Israel its territory 'for ever' don't seem as worried about this second promise, nor about the fourth one we will examine.

However, in 2 Samuel 7:16, the Lord promises King David a perpetual dynasty: 'Your house and your kingdom shall endure for ever before me;

your throne shall be established *for ever.*' However, the kingdom divided as early as the reign of David's grandson, Rehoboam, and the monarchy came to an end in 586 BC. For 2,600 years Israel has been without a king. So we again ask, 'What has happened to the "for ever" promise?'

3. THE CITY

Here is a third 'for ever' promise. In the days of King David, God chose the city of Jerusalem as the location where he would place his name (2 Chr. 6:6). Twice over, he signalled that this would be a permanent arrangement. In 2 Kings 21:7 Manasseh, the king of Judah, is charged with this sin: 'He took the carved Asherah pole he had made and put it in the temple, of which the LORD had said to David and to his son Solomon, "In this temple and in Jerusalem, which I have chosen out of all the tribes of Israel, I will put my Name *for ever.*"' The Chronicler says of Manasseh, 'He built altars in the temple of the LORD, of which the LORD had said, "My Name will remain in Jerusalem *for ever*"' (2 Chr. 33:4).

Yet Jerusalem has not always been the place where the Lord has put his name. The city has had a very chequered history in that regard, and the situation today gives no clue to its having been the city of the Great King. It is currently dominated by a mosque and run by a largely secular government. So what has happened to this 'for ever' promise?

4. THE TEMPLE

The fourth promise has to do with the temple Solomon built. In 1 Kings 9:3, the Lord responds to King Solomon's prayer by saying, 'I have heard the prayer and plea you have made before me; I have consecrated this temple, which you have built, by putting my Name there *for ever.* My eyes and my heart will always be there.'

The temple lasted fewer than four hundred years, being destroyed by Nebuchadnezzar in 586 BC. A second temple was constructed under Zerubbabel upon the return from exile, and a further temple by King

Herod, which was destroyed by the Romans in AD 70. Since that date, Israel has been without a temple. So, once more, we are left asking what happened to the 'for ever' promise.

Where does the problem lie? Does it lie with God? Is his word not reliable? Does he suffer from long-term memory loss? Does he promise something and then fail to come up with the goods? If, however, we cling to God's being thoroughly dependable, what do we do with these 'for ever' promises?

The solution

1. THE OLD COVENANT
The first thing we need to note is that these promises are part of what the New Testament calls 'the Old Covenant'. They pertained while the Old Covenant stood. They applied to the Old Testament people of God.

2. CONDITIONAL PROMISES
The second point we need to note is that all four 'for ever' promises were conditional.

(a) The land
The people of Israel were never given the Promised Land to inhabit as freeholders. It was always theirs to enjoy on leasehold terms so long as they kept the terms of the lease. God said to Israel, '... if you defile the land, it will vomit you out as it vomited out the nations that were before you' (Lev. 18:28). It is hardly surprising that Israel has spent huge periods of time out of the land, and only fully occupied it for a short period of time.

Moreover, in Leviticus 25:23, God said to them, 'The land must not be sold permanently, because the land is mine and you reside in my land as foreigners and strangers.' Hebrews 11 tells us that this was clearly understood in Old Testament times. Unlike the Zionists of today, Abraham 'made his home in the promised land like a stranger in a foreign country' (11:9). In fact, 'All these people ... [admitted] that they were foreigners and strangers on earth' (v. 13).

The land was never theirs as landlords, only as tenants; and that only while they obeyed the Lord.

(b) The monarchy

As for the monarchy, the promise was again conditional. If King David's son, Solomon, didn't walk in the ways of the Lord, he would be disciplined by him; but the Lord had pledged, 'But my love will never be taken away from him' (2 Sam. 7:15). And the Lord kept his word to Solomon, in spite of his rebelliousness. However, he did tear the kingdom from his son Rehoboam (2 Kings 11:29–36; 12:15).

(c) The city

While claiming the city as his own for all time, the Lord again made clear that there were terms to be observed by the people if this was to be a reality. Here they are in 2 Kings, as the Lord responds to Manasseh's crimes:

Therefore this is what the LORD, the God of Israel, says: I am going to bring such disaster on Jerusalem and Judah that the ears of everyone who hears of it will tingle. I will stretch out over Jerusalem the measuring line used against Samaria and the plumb-line used against the house of Ahab. I will wipe out Jerusalem as one wipes out a dish, wiping it and turning it upside-down (2 Kings 21:12–13).

(d) The temple

When it comes to the temple, the very chapter that promised that it would stand for ever as the Lord's house prophesies its destruction in these terms:

But if you or your descendants turn away from me and do not observe the commands and decrees I have given you and go off to serve other gods and worship them, then I will cut off Israel from the land I have given them and will reject this temple I have consecrated for my Name. Israel will then become a byword and an object of ridicule among all peoples. This temple will become a heap of rubble. All who pass by will be appalled and will scoff and say, 'Why has the LORD done such a thing to this land and to this temple?' People will answer, 'Because they have forsaken the LORD their God, who brought their ancestors out of Egypt, and have embraced other gods, worshipping and serving them—that is why the LORD brought all this disaster on them' (1 Kings 9:6–9).

In each of these four cases the 'for ever' promise was conditional. It depended on the people keeping the terms of the promise.

3. THE NEW COVENANT

The final point to note is that these promises have been superseded by something 'better'. We learn from the New Testament that the land of Canaan was a brief foretaste of 'a better country—a heavenly one' (Heb. 11:16). The old monarchy will find its fulfilment in a king of David's line who will not simply rule over a tiny state in the Middle East, but will reign over all the earth: 'Of the increase of his government and peace there will be no end. He will reign on David's throne and over his kingdom, establishing it and upholding it with justice and righteousness from that time on and for ever' (Isa. 9:7). The old Jerusalem will find its fulfilment in the new Jerusalem, the holy city coming down from God out of heaven (Rev. 21:2). And Jerusalem's temple—the meeting place between God and the people—has been replaced by our Lord Jesus Christ. He is now the temple, and always will be (John 2:19–21; Rev. 21:22).

We must read the Old Testament in the light of the New Testament. If we fail to recognize that our Lord and his apostles are the authoritative interpreters of the 'Old', we will be as blind as Jewish or Moslem readers of Old Testament Scripture. We will fail to see the one eternal plan of God to head up everything in Christ through the gospel, shown in the past in what were merely types and shadows of the good things that have now come in Christ.

ABOUT DAY ONE:

Day One's threefold commitment:

- To be faithful to the Bible, God's inerrant, infallible Word;
- To be relevant to our modern generation;
- To be excellent in our publication standards.

I continue to be thankful for the publications of Day One. They are biblical; they have sound theology; and they are relevant to the issues at hand. The material is condensed and manageable while, at the same time, being complete—a challenging balance to find. We are happy in our ministry to make use of these excellent publications.

JOHN MACARTHUR, PASTOR-TEACHER, GRACE COMMUNITY CHURCH, CALIFORNIA

It is a great encouragement to see Day One making such excellent progress. Their publications are always biblical, accessible and attractively produced, with no compromise on quality. Long may their progress continue and increase!

JOHN BLANCHARD, AUTHOR, EVANGELIST AND APOLOGIST

Visit our web site for more information and
to request a free catalogue of our books.
www.dayone.co.uk

Also available

Elisha

Man of mission, Man of miracles

JOHN CHEESEMAN

96PP, PAPERBACK

ISBN 978-1-84625-436-9

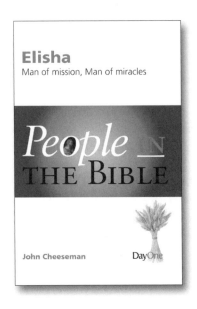

While the life of Elijah is familiar to most Christians, the mission and ministry of his successor, Elisha, is not so well known—probably because of the great drama that surrounded Elijah's service for the Lord. The majority of Elijah's miracles were performed in the context of death and destruction, whereas the miracles of Elisha were mainly to do with healing and restoration. It could therefore be argued that Elijah was primarily a prophet of judgement, whereas his successor was more a prophet of grace. If this is so, the story of Elisha's life is very relevant to the times in which we live. Elisha prophesied in Israel during the ninth century BC as a shining light amid the darkness of idolatry and unbelief which prevailed at the time. We would therefore do well to follow his noble example as we seek to be witnesses for the Lord in our generation.

'Elisha tends to be dwarfed by his great predecessor and mentor, Elijah. But these pages will make you feel you are in the presence of one of the biggest men you have ever met. John Cheeseman has the happy knack of quietly sitting down beside you as you read and saying, "Do you see that?" "Let me explain what the passage means." "Did you notice this?" And his easy style makes each chapter a pleasure to read. As with a good meal, when you finish this book, I think you will be saying "Thanks! I really enjoyed that!"'

SINCLAIR FERGUSON, PROFESSOR OF SYSTEMATIC THEOLOGY AT REDEEMER SEMINARY, DALLAS, TEXAS, AND PART OF THE PREACHING TEAM AT ST PETER'S FREE CHURCH, DUNDEE

Opening Up Ephesians

KURT STRASSNER

160PP, PAPERBACK

ISBN 978-1-84625-437-6

Like Paul's letter to Rome, his letter to the church in Ephesus serves as an invaluable exposition of the Christian gospel. In Ephesians, the apostle has the opportunity simply to explain the riches of the good news, to unfold how the grace of God works in the lives of his people, and to give some basic moral principles. In this commentary, Kurt Strassner conveys the apostle Paul's sheer joy in the riches of the gospel, and provides challenging practical application for Christian living in today's world.

'Kurt Strassner ... helps us understand Paul's own concern in Ephesians: to show how God's revelation of grace in the gospel is of practical relevance for the whole of life.'
IAIN D. CAMPBELL, MINISTER, FREE CHURCH OF SCOTLAND, POINT, ISLE OF LEWIS, AND MODERATOR, GENERAL ASSEMBLY OF THE FREE CHURCH OF SCOTLAND 2012

'An excellent primer for anyone making a foray for the first time into a study of Paul's 'queen of the epistles.' ... Kurt lets the texts talk, and is continually seeking to exalt the Lord Jesus Christ, the one in whom all the spiritual blessings are to be found.'
JOHN SHEARER, SENIOR PASTOR (RETIRED), MUSSELBURGH BAPTIST CHURCH, SCOTLAND

Opening Up
2 Samuel

JIM NEWHEISER

144PP, PAPERBACK

ISBN 978-1-84625-439-0

The book of 2 Samuel centers around the reign of Israel's greatest king, David. Beginning with the record of David's triumphs, it reaches a climax when God establishes His covenant with David in chapter 7. Tragically, when he is at the height of his powers, David commits his great sin with Bathsheba. The latter part of 2 Samuel is a record of the tragic consequences of David's failure. The greatest king Israel ever produced is not good enough. Only the Messiah, the Son of David, will be able to reign in righteousness forever. This commentary gives a brief explanation of the text and then shows how these events have direct and profound application to our lives today, having been recorded "for our instruction" (1 Cor. 10:11). It also reveals how every event points to the coming of Jesus Christ (Luke 24:27), the final and ultimate Leader of God's people.

Opening up
2 Samuel
JIM NEWHEISER
Day One

'We are thankful to God for Jim Newheiser's sure guidance through the twenty-four chapters of 2 Samuel.'
GEOFF THOMAS, ALFRED PLACE BAPTIST CHURCH, ABERYSTWYTH, UK

'The study is deep enough for pastors and teachers, and yet accessible enough for every Christian. I highly recommend it.'
MICHAEL J. KRUGER, REFORMED THEOLOGICAL SEMINARY, USA

Opening Up
Job

IAN S. MCNAUGHTON

176PP, PAPERBACK

ISBN 978-1-84625-437-6

Why do bad things happen to good people? Why me? Can suffering serve any good purpose? These are real questions that many wrestle with today—and that Job wrestled with thousands of years ago. The Book of Job is a historical biography of Job, 'a blameless and upright man', one justified by faith in the sight of God. As it traces his spiritual journey through tragic bereavement and illness, it helps us find solutions to these and other 'hot potato' questions and shows us that sickness and suffering are not always inevitably linked to personal sin.

.

'Revd McNaughton has given us a journey through Job that is both accessible and deeply enriching ... Our attention is continually directed towards Job's Redeemer, who indeed lives.'
STEVE HAM, SENIOR DIRECTOR, ANSWERS IN GENESIS WORLDWIDE

'I am delighted to have read this excellent study on the Book of Job. As a creation speaker, I found the expositions of God's discourse to Job about his creation to be particularly valuable ... I heartily recommend the book.'
PAUL TAYLOR, B.SC., M.ED., DIRECTOR OF MINISTRY DEVELOPMENT, CREATION TODAY, PENSACOLA, FL, USA

Bioethical Issues

Understanding and responding to
the culture of death

JOHN R. LING

320PP, PAPERBACK

ISBN 978-1-84625-427-7

Almost every week the media report
a 'new' bioethical issue. Most people
are confused and unsure about novel
technologies such as saviour siblings,
human cloning, three-parent IVF and
regenerative medicine. Many have
not even thought through the 'old'
bioethical issues of abortion, surrogacy,
infanticide and euthanasia. If that is
your position, this book, fully revised
and updated, is for you. We now live
in a culture of death. Much of modern
medicine has gone seriously wrong. In
its ethics and practices, it has departed
from its historic roots and has therefore
become a threat to all men, women and
children. This book does not seek trite,
comfortable answers. Rather, it develops
a rugged bioethical framework, based
on principles derived from the Bible
and supported by analyses of recent
trends in medicine and science. But this
book is not for cosy, fireside reading. It
wants you out of your chair and doing.
It calls for a head-heart-hand response
of 'principled compassion' to overcome
this culture of death.

'Thoroughly biblical, highly readable, concise yet
remarkably comprehensive—a heartfelt call for
all Christians to engage with bioethics. I hope
many will both read it and respond to it.'
**DR TREVOR STAMMERS, PROGRAMME
DIRECTOR, BIOETHICS AND MEDICAL
LAW, ST MARY'S UNIVERSITY, LONDON**

'While medical advances have brought
innumerable blessings to people in the last
fifty years, they have also spawned a dizzying
world of questions about life and death. John
Ling's *Bioethical Issues* is a welcome help to
navigate these dangerous waters, offering
a map of current medical options, and the
compass of wisdom to discern what is right.'
**DR JOEL R. BEEKE, PRESIDENT OF
PURITAN REFORMED THEOLOGICAL
SEMINARY, GRAND RAPIDS, MICHIGAN**

Our Great God of Wonders

ROGER ELLSWORTH

176PP, PAPERBACK

ISBN 978-1-84625-435-2

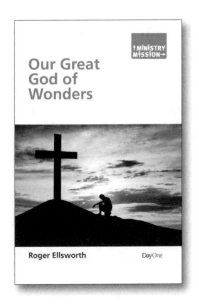

This book is born from the deep-seated conviction that it is vital for Christians to have a good understanding of the doctrinal core of their faith.

The people of God need to understand doctrine, and pastors must lead the way in presenting it.

Not only will such understanding bring comfort and assurance to our hearts, but it will also enable us to stand firmly against the strong forces arrayed against Christianity.

Rejecting the notion that doctrine does not belong in the pulpit, Roger Ellsworth makes Christian theology understandable and interesting for pastors and laypeople alike, with the hope that such understanding will warm our hearts with greater devotion to Christ.

'For many Christians, "doctrine" is an unattractive word, while some belong to a fellowship where the preaching rarely majors on the fundamental facts of the faith. Roger Ellsworth is a sure-footed guide to major issues ranging from before creation to life after death. Pinning everything he says firmly to Scripture, he meticulously traces truth in a way that will surely open minds, warm hearts and strengthen faith. I commend it warmly.'
JOHN BLANCHARD, AUTHOR, EVANGELIST AND CHRISTIAN APOLOGIST

'As I have spent more than thirty-five years with one foot in the local church and one foot in the Christian academy, it does my heart good to find a seasoned pastor writing a book on Christian doctrine. It will benefit the person in the pew and the man behind the pulpit alike. Read it. Pray it. Live it.'
C. BEN MITCHELL, PHD, GRAVES PROFESSOR OF MORAL PHILOSOPHY, UNION UNIVERSITY, JACKSON, TN, USA

Wholeheartedness

The message of Haggai for today

JONATHAN GRIFFITHS

96PP, PAPERBACK

ISBN 978-1-84625-434-5

The great promises of God seem to be only partially fulfilled. The work of the kingdom seems to be moving very slowly, if at all. Unbelievers all around God's people seem to have a better time of it. The people of God are distracted, discouraged & half-hearted in their commitment to the work God has given them to do.

For many believers, that describes our situation & the state of our hearts, just as it describes the situation & the hearts of God's people in Haggai's day. The call of Haggai & of this book is to catch again the vision of God's purposes for His people & the world & to work wholeheartedly at what He has given us to do.

'Here is a clear, careful, faithful and warm exposition of the short book of Haggai. Jonathan's analysis is both deeply encouraging and appropriately challenging. As you read, you will also learn how to understand old-covenant literature in the light of what Christ has done, so you may find yourself doubly blessed.'
ADRIAN REYNOLDS, DIRECTOR OF MINISTRY, THE PROCLAMATION TRUST, UK

'Jonathan Griffiths gives thoughtful attention to details in this Old Testament message without losing sight of the big picture applicable to New Testament Christians. The result is that readers' minds will be informed, their emotions stirred, and their wills challenged to realign their lives with God and his purposes.'
CHARLES PRICE, PREACHER ON THE LIVING TRUTH TELEVISION AND RADIO BROADCASTS

Bible-centred Church

Running a church the biblical way

JOHN TEMPLE

144PP, PAPERBACK

ISBN 978-1-84625-433-8

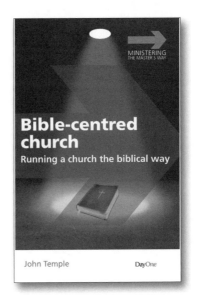

Bible-centred church

Running a church the biblical way

John Temple   DayOne

Most evangelical churches claim to be biblical in all they do. Pastors faithfully encourage their congregations to obey Scripture as their expression of their love for Christ. But does this include the way we structure & run our churches? We all too easily slip into starting with the secular law, tradition or culture, regarding the biblical requirements as 'suggestions', yet it is the Bible that should be our starting point. We should endeavour to 'render to Caesar the things that are Caesar's' & observe those elements of secular law, tradition or culture which are not in conflict with the Bible, but reject anything that is contrary to the Bible.

Using a scale from 'Precepts' (the Ten Commandments) to 'Freedoms' (issues on which the Bible is silent), this book provides practical advice on how to apply the Bible to church organisation.

'John Temple offered biblical insight to our congregation as we made the transition to elder leadership. This book is written from a divine perspective and is saturated in practical application. It may not be your only resource for biblical church polity, but it will be the best!'
DR REGGIE WEEMS, PASTOR, HERITAGE BAPTIST CHURCH, JOHNSON CITY, TN, USA

'This book seeks to deal with very real, concrete and specific issues, and it seeks to do so from a distinctly biblical perspective.'
DR WAYNE MACK, PASTOR/ELDER AT LYNNWOOD BAPTIST CHURCH AND PROFESSOR OF BIBLICAL COUNSELLING AT STRENGTHENING MINISTRIES TRAINING INSTITUTE, PRETORIA, SOUTH AFRICA